MW00977183

Naked Sex

For Married Couples Only

By

Oscar & Crystal Jones

Naked Sex

For Married Couples Only

By

Oscar & Crystal Jones

Destiny House Publishing, LLC
Detroit, MI

Naked Sex
For Married Couples Only

Published by Destiny House Publishing, LLC

Copyright July 2012 Oscar & Crystal Jones

International Standard Book Number:
ISBN-13: 978-1936867233

Unless otherwise stated, all scripture quotations are from the
Holy Bible, King James Version

Scripture references that do not have the Bible version noted are
the author's paraphrase.

Original printing 2012

Cover design. Editing and Publication Layout:

Destiny House Publishing, LLC

Artwork: Dreamstime, Inc.

Printed in the United States of America

For information:
Destiny House Publishing, LLC
www.destinyhousepublishing.com
P.O. Box 19774 - Detroit, MI 48219
888.890.9455

Acknowledgments & Dedications

We would like to acknowledge first and foremost, our Lord and Savior, Jesus Christ. We are honored to be in his service and have the awesome privilege of writing this book.

We dedicate this book to our married children

Jake & Keila Allen
Erik & Charity Dean

And to the young marrieds in our lives:

Gregory & Saryta Colbert
James & Bobby Jean Curry
Darnell & RaSheedah Deboes
John & Serena Eagen
Timashion & Tavia Jones
Andre & Jessica Murphy
Esosa & Shereena Osai
Tvo & LaQuitia Robinson
Jonathan & Bessie Sims
Therian & Cathy Smith
Christopher & Joyce Willis
Anthony & Aries Winans
Randy & Ticie Winans

NAKED SEX

CHAPTERS

CHAPTER ONE
LET'S GET DOWN & FLIRTY

-ONE-
LET'S GET DOWN & FLIRTY

A loving doe, a graceful deer — may her breasts satisfy you always, may you ever be intoxicated with her love.
Proverbs 5:19 NIV

When you get right down to it, sex is just good. There is nothing dull or dirty or unholy about it. It feels good, it sounds good, and it **is** good. It was God's idea, but we act as if we have to hide it from Him. Let's set the record straight. It is not improper to talk about sex. God is not covering his eyes and turning his head when we connect physically. He doesn't tip out the room. He is quite interested in our sex lives. It's time we invited him in.

This book is written to get to the heart of the matter. Married people have been too timid in talking about such an important subject.

Sex is the topic that we are most interested in but for some reason, we seem to shy away from it. Not only do we neglect teaching on the subject in the church, married couples have reservations about talking about it to their spouses. Oh sure, we will set the time and place. But we seem to blush when encouraged to talk about what we like and don't like. Our faces flush and we lower our heads.

We have shhh'ed each other far too many times. It's time to come out with it. Married people have questions and lots of them. So it is our aim to deal with this nearly taboo-ish subject from a healthy perspective. What was God thinking when He created such a beautiful and intimate act?

Let's talk about it.

Let's search the scriptures on it. We hope that after reading this book, you will feel liberated to enjoy a more satisfying relationship with your spouse.

We have prayed over this book and over every person who picks this book up. May the Spirit of the Living God connect you and your spouse at a deeper level and cause you to experience the type of intimacy that few marriages do.

Let go of your bashfulness. Step out of your preconceived notions. Come to the table with an empty plate ready to receive. Let God paint you a picture of all that you've been missing. Let's judge our ideals by the Word and not what we've overheard.

So take a deep breath. Let's dig into God's heart and get on with it.

At the end of the book, there is a chapter on frequently asked questions. We wanted to take all those questions that have been sitting, baking in your hearts for years. You know those questions that you were too embarrassed to ask your pastor (or any leader for that matter). Well, fear no longer. No one will look at you funny or get the wrong impression. We have taken the toughest questions – on oral sex, sex toys, etc. And we have answered every one. It's all there. And if we've missed any, feel free to contact us. We will get the answer to you. Our email address is in the back as well.

We hope to alleviate your doubts. We pray that you will get a clear understanding of God's original motive for sex. We hope that you will not only grow in your own relationship but that you will be able to help others when asked. We have an obligation to offer godly counsel, not our own opinion.

As married couples, let's have loads and loads of sex with our spouses. Let's laugh and run through the house naked. Do it in different rooms of the house. Try new positions. Talk sexy to one another. Probe each other's body. Let's make God smile. After all, it was his idea, in the first place.

CHAPTER TWO
PURE SEX

-TWO-
PURE SEX

Marriage should be honored by all, and the marriage bed kept pure, for God will judge the adulterer and all the sexually Hebrews 13:4 NIV

The LORD God said, "It is not good for the man to be alone. I will make a helper suitable for him."

Now the LORD God had formed out of the ground all the wild animals and all the birds in the sky. He brought them to the man to see what he would name them; and whatever the man called each living creature, that was its name. So the man gave names to all the livestock, the birds in the sky and all the wild animals.

But for Adam no suitable helper was found. So the LORD God caused the man to fall into a deep sleep; and while he was sleeping, he took one of the man's ribs and then closed up the place with flesh. Then the LORD God made a woman from the rib he had taken out of the man, and he brought her to the man. The man said,

"This is now bone of my bones
and flesh of my flesh;
she shall be called 'woman,'
for she was taken out of man."

That is why a man leaves his father and mother and is united to his wife, and they become one flesh.

Adam and his wife were both naked, and they felt no shame. Genesis 2:18-25 NIV

It's quite interesting that when God gifted Adam with this woman, he knew exactly what to do with her. God didn't have to talk him through it. He needed no pictures, no instructions. He saw her body and immediately he knew what went where. The two became one physically as a natural example of what was to happen spiritually. And they did. We imagine that God was well pleased.

He presented Eve to Adam in the buff. Neither of them needed covering. Their nakedness represented: intimacy, innocence, and freedom. This was God's desire for mankind.

Man would have **intimacy** with God and intimacy with his wife in that nothing would be hidden. No secrets, no masks. What you see would be exactly what you would get. In this pre-fallen state, Eve had no insecurities about her body. Her size and shape did not matter. Both the man and his wife had their healthy self-image neatly tucked away in God. All that mattered was the love and attraction they had for God and for one another.

Their **innocence** was that they knew no sin. They had no capacity to harm the other. Their knowledge was limited. They had pure motives. They lacked experience in manipulation and control.

Their sexual encounter was free of perversion, lust, anger and all the sins that make sex unpleasant.

Their **freedom** was an amazing gift. They were free to love uninhibitedly. They could swing from the trees and run through the grass frolicking in the meadow; feeding each other fruit while lying in the sun. This was their space that the Lord had created especially for the two of them and He wanted them to enjoy one another. There were no worries. No lack. No pain. Pure, unadulterated freedom.

This was the perfect setting. Adam and Eve had it made; a God who loved them more than anything, just the two of them in the world, no competitors for each other's attention. No bosses, no instructors, no neighbors. All the sex they wanted in the most beautiful garden in the world, every desire at their fingertips. What more could they have asked for?

Unfortunately, there was an intruder in the garden. The slick infiltrator slithered in, offering doubt, insecurities, lust, rebellion, and perversion in exchange for their liberty. The poisoned fruit was a temptation they did not resist. And with that the couple had to be covered. *Their nakedness was gone.* Lost. They had negotiated their nakedness for something far lesser in value. It cost them more than they bargained for. They would no longer enjoy the intimacy they once had with God. Their own closeness was diminished as they begin to accuse. To top it off, neither of them was innocent and they were now banned from the garden where they enjoyed so much freedom.

And today sex isn't as beautiful as it once was. Our culture is inundated with it. We don't respect or appreciate this gift that God presents to a man and his wife on their wedding night. Today, we prematurely engage in sex. We disregard the Lord's warning about opening this gift too soon. Statistics say the majority of Americans engage in premarital sex. We misuse it. We sell it, manipulate to get it, and we try to impress others with how much of it we get. We take it from those who don't want to give it to us. We advertise our products with it. We mock those who want to hold on to it until marriage.

Certainly, we've lost the awe of it. There is a thrill lost that God intended that we experience as we venture into covenant. It was part of the gift. Think about it, if both husband and wife's first sexual experience was on their wedding night, how might that have changed their sexual relationship?

What if we didn't have all the cultural biases in our head? What if we had no other memories or soul ties? What if we had not ever known fornication, pornography, molestation, rape, or any abuse? What if we only knew pure sex? No images. No additives. No muss, no fuss. What would pure sex feel like? It almost seems farfetched, sort of unattainable in this world we live in.

We would like to propose to you that *Pure Sex* is attainable. Things that are impossible with men are possible with God. The Lord is able to deliver and set you free from the soul ties and memories that bind you. If you struggle with pornographic images, the Lord wants you to start with a clean slate with your spouse. Don't take the polluted sexual experiences of your past into your future. You can start again. God has the amazing ability to renew our minds. And they do need renewing.

With advertising, innuendos, and covert sexual messages in nearly every program that comes from Hollywood and Madison Avenue, we have a battle to fight. And it is definitely in our minds.

Thinking About Pure Sex

A person can hardly escape 24 hours where there is not some image or reference made to illicit sexual relationships. Our culture glorifies it, to make it more acceptable and slips it into our consciousness.

So as believers, we step into marriage not really knowing what is suitable. Most young couples drag whatever sexual hang-ups they had pre "I do" right into the marriage. Many couples were involved in fornication before they were married not fully comprehending that lust is a spirit. Saying "I do" doesn't deliver one from a spirit of lust. Unbeknown to the couple, the spirit of lust is dragged right into the marriage. It is transformed from fornication, it is revealed as a porn addiction, flirtation, voyeurism or even adultery in the relationship.

So how do we get to pure sex in marriage?

Couples should take time to repent of their premarital sins to God and to one another. Be honest about ungodly thoughts and images that clutter your mind during your time of physical intimacy.

- Begin with a heart of repentance. Repent to God for any idols that have staked a claim on your heart. Then repent to your spouse for prior sexual experiences if you both were not sexually pure when you came to the marriage. Understand being a virgin and being sexually pure are two very different states. A person can be a virgin who engaged in heavy petting, masturbation, dry humping and other lewd acts. However a person who is sexually pure has kept his/her body and mind holy. Sexual purity begins in the thoughts, not the body. You do not have to give each other details about your past; just clear the air. Make a promise to give yourself fully to the other.

- Seek deliverance from lust and sexual addictions. Ask God to purify your sexual relationship.

- Be committed to it. Keep your thoughts on one another. Do not watch "X" or and some "R" rated movies (for sexual content). Evict all the images in your mind from soft and hard core porn. Decide you will not allow yourself to view any such images going forward. When you are with your spouse be fully present. Don't allow your mind to go to some movie, memory or visual from your past. Let your spouse be enough. The more you bring images into your bed, the more distance you create between you and your spouse. You will have a hard time connecting the way God wants because you have allowed a spirit of lust to control your mind. Thus, the image becomes more important than connecting with your mate.

- Clear out any old lingerie, gifts, scents, etc. from an ex-lover. You should also shred old pictures and love letters from your ex. Discard all magazines, movies, and music that do not project a holy image.

- Couples usually avoid sex talk, but it is vital for a healthy relationship. Talk about your fears and struggles with each other. Also, talk about what you enjoy. It really is okay for the two of you to talk about your sex.

- Invite God into your bedroom. It is really a good thing to pray before sex! Ask God to bless your time of intimacy (remember sex was God's idea). You may find yourself more relaxed and free to enjoy your spouse. Thank God afterward, as well.

Let's make pure sex a priority in our unions. Let's reclaim our nakedness.

CHAPTER THREE
PLEASURE ME

-THREE-
PLEASURE ME

May your fountain be blessed, and may you rejoice in the wife of your youth. A loving doe, a graceful deer--may her breasts satisfy you always, may you ever be captivated by her love. Proverbs 5:18, 19 NIV

Sex in Christian marriage is meant to bring pleasure to both spouses not just solely for the husband or for the wife. This whole "two becoming one" idea invokes selflessness. It's about serving one another. It should not be sex for one. The complete act of sex is communion of two self-giving adults.

The husband should fulfill his marital duty to his wife, and likewise the wife to her husband. The wife's body does not belong to her alone but also to her husband. In the same way, the husband's body does not belong to him alone but also to his wife. I Corinthians 7:3-4

The married couple's bodies belong to them both. Both equally share in the possession of the other. The wife's body is hers but she alone cannot make decisions for it. And the same goes for the husband. In order for one to have pleasure the other must agree.

Sex was not meant to be at the expense of the other spouse. Neither spouse can demand pleasure from the other. It must be in unison and consensual. We get and give sex to each other. Never should sex be one-sided with an unwilling partner. At that point, it is ungodly.

Selfishness just does not work in marriage. We cannot be interested in only our own desires. A healthy sexual relationship happens when both spouses are concerned with pleasing the other. We have to get to the place where we understand that sex in Christian marriage is not for your enjoyment alone, it's meant to be enjoyable for **both** spouses. Like everything else in your life, it should not dishonor God.

Some have the point of view that the husband can demand sex from his wife because he is the head. This notion is not supported by scripture. It is selfish for a husband to insist that his needs be fulfilled simply because he is the head. As he ministers to his wife, she will minister to him. It's a dance of sorts. He steps toward her and she steps with him. God is never pleased when we operate in selfishness.

Some further assert that Paul insisted that the wife not withhold sex from her husband, which therefore gives him the right to it.

Let us examine said scripture:

Do not deprive **each other** except perhaps by **mutual consent** and for a time, so that you may devote yourselves to prayer. Then come together again so that Satan will not tempt you because of your lack of self-control. I Corinthians 7:5 NIV (bold emphasis ours)

Certainly, husband and wife should not regularly practice withholding themselves from each other. Wives must be especially careful, as some tend to lash out in anger, using sex to barter for an apology or some other good behavior. It is wrong for either spouse to decide that she/he will not be intimate with their partner as a punishment. This is not the will of God. Sex was not meant to be used as a weapon, manipulative tool, or as a means of control. Sex is holy and good and should never ever be used for evil.

God intended that the two come together frequently for sex. This creates a strong bond between husband and wife.

However, Paul continues in verse 6 "I say this as a concession, not as a command." He gives us a principle in keeping the marriage bed holy but he also says this is not written in stone. There are times when a wife is simply **unable** to have sex with her husband. Her husband needs to be understanding about this.

Such times include if she…

> has an illness,
> is exhausted
> is menstruating,
> has given birth,

has had surgery,
is bleeding emotionally
has vaginal pain/dryness

A wise husband will be sensitive to his wife. Tend to her. Bring her a heating pad, run her a hot bath, and rub her back. Get her some meds. Help her to feel better. When she has recovered, he will be greatly rewarded for his patience and genuine concern. If he is sowing love and care for his wife, he is sure to reap a harvest of love and care back to himself.

In those times when a couple cannot engage in intercourse, but "both" still want to connect sexually, there are still ways to be sexual with one another. Touching, fondling, cuddling, and kissing are all ways to engage your spouse.

The wife can get satisfied emotionally while she is satisfying her husband physically. She can offer her husband a quickie. A quickie is when a wife helps her husband to an ejaculation or husband strokes his wife's clitoris to bring her to orgasm. The wife can stroke her husband's penis and scrotal area to bring him to ejaculation with her hand. Or it could be a quick sexual encounter complete with a lubricated condom to take away the mess. It is far more common for wives to give a quickie to their husbands just because the way men and women are wired sexually.

When a couple is in their childbearing season, the husband often has to wait months before sex gets put back on the table. Some women cannot tolerate sex in the last month of pregnancy. And then after she has the baby, add another 6 weeks (or more) to that timeline. That husband can be more than a little frustrated. In those cases, a wife can help her husband out. No demands on his part. No control. Husband and wife should naturally desire to show love for each other and so they agree. Wife can enjoy the cuddling and closeness; and husband can enjoy the physical release of their non-vaginal sexual experience.

The most important thought we would like to communicate is be creative and selfless. Explore each other's bodies in non-traditional ways.

CHAPTER FOUR
MAKING LOVE TO YOUR WIFE

-FOUR-
MAKING LOVE TO YOUR WIFE

The husband's body does not belong to him alone but also to his wife. I Corinthians 7:4b

Husbands we are to love our wives with everything in us. Sometimes that's more easily said than done. But, we can learn to love her. Making love to our wives is something that we must do on a continual basis. I don't mean the actual physical act; but loving her with your thoughts.

Making love starts with your attitude.

It starts in your head. How do you feel about your wife? Have you allowed unresolved issues to linger in your heart? How do you feel about yourself? These questions and many more come to mind as you seek to make love to your wife. Start with loving thoughts. Thoughts that bring joy to your heart. Satan would love for you to meditate on the issues of the day. But choose to think loving thoughts and watch how that can be transformed into great lovemaking.

Make sure she's not exhausted and overwhelmed. Help out with the chores and the children. This will allow her to have more energy for you.

She will need to feel relaxed. Make sure there is a lock on your door for tiny prowlers who don't always knock.

Men are aroused by sight, so it is sometimes hard for a man to understand the need of this process of emotional attachment. People are usually attached to themselves. We love ourselves. Therefore, just like we emotionally attach to ourselves, men are to become emotionally attached with their wives.

Overcoming selfishness is the key to making love to your wife. Men are moved by sight, so we must consciously and on purpose work on our emotions. Let me get this straight. Men are emotional; we just display it in different ways. We aren't in touch with our emotions in the same way as our wives. So we will need to put in more work.

In order to effectively make love to her, you must connect on that emotional level. There are many different things you can do from a tangible perspective to connect with her. Say sexy things to her throughout the day. Call her during the day to see how she is doing and tell her you can't wait to see her that night. Wash the dishes, make the bed, arrange for a babysitter or do something you wouldn't normally do. Be creative, and set the tone to connect with her.

Once you have learned how to love your wife emotionally, you are free to explore the other areas of making love to her.

When you have connected with her on that

level you will be free to roam around the cabin, so to speak. Watch for signs that give you permission from your wife to go to other areas you both might enjoy.

Pregame Warm-up

As you began to explore those other areas you must understand the dynamics of male and female sexuality. It has been said before when it comes to sex, men are like microwaves and women are like slow cookers. There is a lot of truth to that. Women require foreplay in order to get in the mood most of the time. Men just require a place.

Foreplay can start as early as morning. It's like a salad; it is part of the meal. It is not the main course but it is an important part of the meal.

As stated earlier, connecting with your wife can be the initial part of foreplay. Start with things you know that turn your wife on in the morning and work those things all day. Cook her breakfast. Create an atmosphere where she can't wait until you get home. Text her throughout the day and be as graphic as you can without being offensive.

During the pregame warm-up of a sports game you are stretching and flexing your muscles to get them ready to perform. It's similar in the sexual experience. She performs better when she is warmed up. So do not rush the pregame to get the best performance. Once she is warm she usually will let you know. You can follow her lead from there on.

Then begin to caress and touch. Remember, she is a tender flower and must be handled gently.

Entering the game.

As you began to make love to your wife, don't rush through it. Don't do the bare minimum just to get to your orgasm. Be sensitive to your wife. It's easy for men to just go for it. Men have to be careful not to become selfish. Take your time with her. Talk to her and say things you know will turn her on. Be gentle with her. Don't go banging around like you have a hammer and you are trying to drive a nail in a wood plank. Be sensitive to her. Make love to her body and her mind.

Sometimes, a husband may become overly excited, especially if his wife is moaning. Fight off the temptation to rush it just because you hear her moan. Control your mind, so that you don't experience a premature ejaculation; leaving her disappointed and unsatisfied. Work to temper your emotions. Slow down. You really can control it. But it takes work.

There are exercises you can do to gain control of your orgasm.
Outside of your sexual experience practice Kegel exercises. Halfway through urination, try to stop or slow down the flow of urine. Don't tense the muscles in your buttocks, legs, or abdomen, and don't hold your breath. When you can slow or stop

the flow of urine, you've successfully located these muscles. Contract these muscles for a slow count of five. Release the muscles to a slow count of five. Repeat 10 times. Do a set of 10 daily, three times a day. This will cause you to gain more control sexually.

However, if for some reason you are in that learning stage and you do reach an orgasm without your wife, don't just leave her hanging. Continue in the sexual experience. Help her to enjoy the experience. Find out what she would like you to do, when/if that happens.

One thing men really need to understand is that a woman does not need an orgasm in order to enjoy sex. You should not put unreasonable demands on your wife. Some men tend to put enormous pressure on their wives because it is affirmation to their egos when she does reach an orgasm. Others feel rejected or like they have failed.

However, if a husband understands that all women do not experience orgasm (contrary to what's depicted on television or in the movies); he will have a much more enjoyable experience. If your wife is one who does experience orgasms, she will not experience them every time you have sex. So be okay with that. She can still receive pleasure from the experience. Many wives have faked orgasms just to satisfy the egos of their husbands.

Offer her variety. Don't do the same thing every time. Change it up. She will like something one day but that same thing won't do it for her the next week. Women are finicky about sex. It's your job to figure her out. And you really have a lifetime to do it. So read her signals. It's going to mean you will have to pay attention. Even if she tells you she likes something, don't keep doing that same thing over and over again.

Women are especially sensitive to smells. A strong odor could be a turnoff for her. Make sure that you bathe and brush your teeth when approaching her. The sexual experience is more enjoyable for her if she is not repulsed by your body odor. When you are planning a sexual interlude, watch what you eat as well. Passing gas in the bedroom might evoke humor to you, but it can be very offensive to your wife. Men and women are different that way.

CHAPTER FIVE
MAKING LOVE TO YOUR HUSBAND

-FIVE-
MAKING LOVE TO YOUR HUSBAND

The wife's body does not belong to her alone but also to her husband. I Corinthians 7:4a

We encourage husbands and wives to begin their lovemaking with prayer. It may sound a little unusual, but it is very important. Prayer invites God into your bedroom; and allows you the opportunity to engage in pure sex without all the negative stuff from your past. Prayer helps you both with the issues of premature ejaculation and sexual frustration. God is able and willing to help you in those areas. Ask Him to bless your experience.

Set the atmosphere for your husband. Your bedroom should be clean and neat. If you have children or other dependents, you should make sure that there is a lock on your bedroom door. There is nothing like being walked in on while you are having sex. For about $25 at the local hardware store, you can have peace of mind and your children won't be freaked out.

Create an environment in your bedroom that awakens his senses and yours. Engage all 5 senses.

Smell: Use linen spray on your bed. Choose your favorite candle or incense fragrance. Make sure you also smell good with perfume or body spray.

Taste: Feel free to bring in foods that stimulate you sexually; chocolate sauce, chocolate covered strawberries, whipped cream, etc.

Sight: Wear your sexiest lingerie, even if you don't like it. Remember it's not for you. Men are visual. He is not interested in your comfy flannel pajamas. Save those for a non-sexual time.

When you are having unplanned sex (no time for lingerie), you should aim for naked sex. Take off all of your clothes, don't leave on your pajama top or socks. Let him enjoy your entire body. That means you cannot be opposed to keeping the lights on while you are making love. Women often struggle with body image. But your husband gets excited about seeing your naked body. Let him enjoy you. Allow him to examine you. This is his body, too. Break out of the mode that the lights have to be off.

Touch: Bring in massage oils. Caress your husband's body. Take your time. Do not rush through the process. Start with the foot or neck and work your way to his genitals. If you have purchased edible oils, you may want to use your mouth to arouse him. Understand that your husband needs to be desired. It is perfectly fine for you to initiate sex. Most men are turned on when a wife initiates foreplay or sex.

Hear: Pillow talk is important. Talk to him while you are caressing his body. Talk sexy, not dirty. Some couples use profanity in the bedroom. We highly discourage this. Curse words are words from your polluted past. This is how you approached sex before you understood that God had another idea. So by all means talk to your spouse. Incite him with your words. But avoid profanity. He also needs to be affirmed during the love making process. His self image is tied to the sexual experience. So praise him. Your words are very important. Stroke his ego. Be generous with your praise. Tell him how much you enjoy what he is doing. Do not tell him what he is doing wrong. You shouldn't give off any negative signals during the love making process. Gently guide him, if he is going in the wrong direction. Discuss at a later (nonsexual) time the things you do not like.

If your spouse enjoys music, by all means, bring soft romantic music in your bedroom.

Do not leave the television on while you are making love. It is a distraction. Don't just mute it. It's a good idea to cut the television off. Concentrate on one another.

Do not allow your sex life to become a burden or a duty to perform. Don't have sex with your spouse out of guilt. Your husband not only wants you. He wants you to want to be with him. His need for sex is not just physical. His ability to pleasure his wife is important to his confidence as a man. It is an important emotional need. If you struggle in the area of wanting to have sex with your husband, ask the Lord to help you in this area. You want to fully immerse yourself in the experience. It is a blessing to have a husband with a healthy sex drive. Do not take that for granted. You should also revel in the fact that he wants to have sex with his wife. Give yourself to him. Relax and enjoy your husband's body. Bask in the closeness. Feel his love for you and affirm him in the process.

When you deny him sex, he feels rejected. A husband may sometimes feel like you are not interested in him. Going through the motions isn't enough to affirm him. A wife must be fully involved and not come to the marriage bed annoyed. You cannot love him as a husband but reject him sexually. He wants to connect with you.

There may be times when you just do not feel like having sex. However you should not withhold yourself from your spouse. Remember love is absent of selfishness. So sometimes you can make it just about him. "Bless" your husband. Make yourself available for him. Certain positions you can agree will be for his pleasure only. A quickie will help him out when you may not have time for the full experience. You get satisfied emotionally because you are satisfying your husband physically. Make sure you are emotionally engaged even if it's just a quickie.

Some women have a hard time relaxing because of the fear of pregnancy. If you are not ready to have a baby, make sure that you agree upon the type of birth control that you will use. Talk to your doctor, about the choices available to you. Then you and husband should make the best decision for the two of you.

There may be times when a husband struggles with premature ejaculation. This is especially common in young marriages. A wife should not make her husband feel bad if she finds herself in this experience. He does not want this to happen. He hasn't learned yet how to temper his arousal. If a wife puts her husband down or constantly condemns him, she will find herself locked in a vicious cycle. Because the worse he feels, the more he will have anxiety about it. Often as he has tension about it, he sometimes will experience a lost erection for fear of a premature ejaculation.

A wife should practice patience so that she can help her husband relax and work with her husband to develop their sexual relationship. The more he relaxes the better control he will have over his orgasm. However, if he feels like a failure, most often, he will continue to fail. (As a man thinks in his heart, so is he).

The wise wife will reassure her husband that he will have plenty of opportunities to finish what he started. They have a whole life together to work on their sexual relationship. The two are both learning and growing. Additionally, there are other things she could have him do to help her enjoy the sexual encounter and/or reach her orgasm.

When a wife is fully satisfied in the sexual experience, she should thank her husband. A man's ego and sexuality are strongly connected. Showing appreciation to him helps him in his sexuality. He feels confident and strong. When men are appreciated or celebrated, they are anxious to return to that area of the marriage. So offer generous appreciation and offer it often.

CHAPTER SIX
WHERE THE WILD THINGS ARE

WHERE THE WILD THINGS ARE

You are tall and supple, like the palm tree, and your full breasts are like sweet clusters of dates. I say, "I'm going to climb that palm tree! I'm going to caress its fruit!" Oh yes! Your breasts will be clusters of sweet fruit to me, Your breath clean and cool like fresh mint. Song of Solomon 7:7,8MSG

Adam and Eve had sex on the ground in the tall grass or maybe under a tree. There is something a little wild about that. Sex in its original unpolluted state had a wild side to it. Even as sin has caused us to lose our nakedness, we've lost some of our wild side. Somehow we have religionized sex. We've contained it. We want to have sex in our bed at night in the dark. We think that is most spiritual. Sex is most definitely a spiritual experience. But let's take the religion (man-made ideas and rules) out of it. Certainly there is a line drawn in relating sexually with your spouse. There are things that God clearly opposes in scripture. Those things are outlined in the next chapter. However, it is clear that God intended that a man and his wife would thoroughly enjoy one another. It's time we stirred up that wild side in our natures, release our inhibitions, and step outside of our comfort zone. We will surprise our spouses …and maybe even ourselves.

Positions: The missionary position is not the only "acceptable" position. You and your spouse should feel free to experiment with different positions. However, whatever position you want to try out, make sure your spouse is comfortable with it. Do not attempt to coerce your spouse to participate in something that makes him/her uneasy. The objective is to have fun and enjoy one another. So go ahead and try new things, but make sure you both agree. Certainly you will want to avoid those positions that are painful to the wife.

Dance for your spouse. Husbands and wives both may enjoy this one. But men especially will enjoy seeing their wives dance seductively. Choose appropriate music. Praise and worship may not do it for you. Secular music is okay as long as you make sure the words line up with scripture. The Bible says words are spirit. So avoid music that promotes adultery, threesomes, etc.

She may even want to shed layers of clothing as the music continues. Or her husband may want her to just dance naked. You don't have to be a good dancer to do this. He will just enjoy the show.

Games. Play the strip version of your favorite game. For each round, the loser must take off a garment of clothing until one or both of you are completely naked. From there, just use your imagination. Have fun!

Role play. It's okay if your wife dresses

provocatively in the bedroom. Make your love life exciting. Act out your fantasies within reason (refer to next chapter). She may want to dress in a sexy maid outfit. He may want to wear nothing but cowboy boots and a hat. Go for it!

Try new places. Certainly we don't want anyone getting arrested. It is illegal to have sex in public places. However don't just confine sex to the boudoir. Have sex in the shower, kitchen, on the couch, in a tent in your backyard, etc. You get the drift. Just make sure there are no witnesses present.

Don't just do it at night. Rush home for a mid morning rendezvous. Make love in the afternoon. Greet each other in the morning with some a.m. passion. Break out of your routine.

And whatever you do, do not broadcast your sex life. Keep it private. This is just between you and your mate. You don't want to give anyone any ideas. They may think they want what you have, literally. It has happened before. It's good decorum to keep your relationship quiet. So if you swing from the ceiling fan, just keep it between the two of you.

Have fun. Enjoy each other, but if you or your spouse feels dirty, disrespected, or degraded after sex then something is seriously wrong in your bedroom. It's time to talk about it and make the appropriate adjustments.

~~~

If you struggle with knowing what is acceptable and what is not, here are some myths that we hope will help your understanding and free you in the bedroom.

Sex Myth #1 Sex drive disappears after age 50. Age is relative. It depends on the person. A couple can have a very healthy and active sex life even at 60 and 70. We encourage couples to not surrender their sex life just because they are older. There are many options to help you with your sexuality. Continually pray for a healthy sex life and be thankful for the sex life you do enjoy.

Sex Myth #2 My spouse should know how to please me sexually. This is certainly false. But many couples act as if it's true. We make love to our spouses day after day and for years without ever sharing what we like and dislike. For some strange reason we believe our mates should get this information by osmosis.

Women are especially guilty of this one. They often think their husband's knowledge of them should be automatic, even though most times he has proven them wrong time and time again. The fact of the matter is your husband is not omniscient. If you don't tell him what feels good or what you dislike sexually, then he will never know. And you will consistently be frustrated.

Sex Myth #3 The wife should never initiate sex. This is also false. Traditionally, Christian women and some men have been taught that when it comes to sex, the wife should never initiate. This inhibits many couples. A husband needs to feel desired by his wife. Most men feel especially turned on when approached by their wives. It is perfectly acceptable for a wife to initiate sex with her husband. It builds her husband's ego and self-image. Go for it ladies.

Sex Myth #4 Sex is only for procreation. This is certainly not true. Physical intimacy is a vital part of the marriage covenant. All couples do not have the ability to have children. So should they abstain from sex? God created sex with pleasure in mind. Married couples should feel free to enjoy sex even without the idea of conceiving.

Sex Myth #5 It is not permissible for Christians to experiment in the bedroom. This makes no sense. Couples have to keep their sex life passionate and exciting. This requires that they try new things (within the confines of scripture).

Sex Myth #6 There is only one sexual position that is holy – missionary position. The Bible does not hail the missionary position as holier than any other. In fact, the Bible is silent on positions. The missionary position is often uncomfortable for pregnant women in the last trimester. So it is a good idea for couples to find what works for them.

Sex Myth #7 Married couples should have sex several times a week. Every person is different. People have different sex drives and are at different seasons of their lives. Each marriage must set its own sexual rhythm. Some couples may have sex once a week. While others may come together 2-3 times a week. Some couples have sex every once in a while. Either way, as long as both spouses are content with their frequency, that is all that matters. There is no set rule. So don't fall into the trap of comparing yourself to others.

Sex Myth #8 The husband is the head in the bedroom, and so the wife must do whatever he says. It is true that the wife is subject to her husband; however the Bible also says that the husband's body belongs not to him alone but to the wife as well. Scripture also admonishes us to submit to one another. Love isn't forceful or selfish. Love is kind.

Sex Myth #9 Men want sex all of the time. So not true. Our culture gives us the image that men are always ready to jump in the bed. This is a myth, ladies. Sometimes it's the husband who is putting his wife off. While statistics say men usually have higher sex drives then their wives, it is not always the case. In our counseling experiences, we have seen the higher drive with the wives.

CHAPTER SEVEN
FORBIDDEN FRUIT

-SEVEN-
FORBIDDEN FRUIT

Drink water from your own well -- share your love only with your wife. Why spill the water of your springs in public, having sex with just anyone? You should reserve it for yourselves. Don't share it with strangers. Proverbs 5:15-17NLT

With very little teaching on sex in the church environment, many Christian married couples worry about what is allowed and what is not allowed in the bedroom. We want you to understand that sex in and of itself is good. It was God's design. And used within its boundaries it is a blessing to a married couple. However, when we use something for some other purpose than what it was intended, it is met with formidable consequences. God intended sex to be a beautiful symphony of two becoming one in their thoughts, emotions, and physical bodies. This type of intimacy evokes a godly soul tie between husband and wife. It's the glue that causes marriages to flourish for a lifetime. God's intent was and still is for couples to fully enjoy one another. The beauty of sex is demonstrated in the book of Song of Solomon.

It is the binding of two spirits, minds, and bodies into one. No others can be included in that process. Neither should one spouse decide to simply engage in sex alone (masturbation and pornography). Sex was meant to be much more than physical stimulation. It's the two coming together as one producing intimacy in the relationship.

God designed sex to exist within certain boundaries. Sex is pleasing within its boundaries of holiness. It is beautiful and sacred. However when it is outside of God's purpose, sex is damaging and harmful.

Below is a list of sexual behaviors that do not glorify God and are harmful to your marriage:

Adultery, Swinging, Threesomes, Pedophilia. This is sex with someone other than or including your spouse. Matthew 5:28. (Deut 5:18, Prov 6:32, Hebrews 13:4) I Corinthians 7:2, 4

Bestiality - Sex with animals (Exodus 22:19, Leviticus 20:15-16)

Homosexuality/lesbianism – sex with someone of the same sex. Leviticus 20:13, Leviticus 18:22, Romans 1:26-27

Incest- sex with a relative / family member. See Leviticus 18:7-18; 20:11-21.

Pornography- Sexual Images Matt 5:27-28, Romans 1:32

Prostitution: Paying for sex. See Leviticus 19:29, Deuteronomy 23:17, and Proverbs 7:4-27.

Rape - Forced sex without consent. See Deuteronomy 22:25, 28

Voyeurism - watching other people have sex or

watching their naked bodies Matt 5:27-28, Romans 1:32

This list is certainly not exhaustive. We want to make sure that our sexual experience is consistent with God's original idea. Even though we want you to feel free in your sexual expression, **we don't want you to think that anything goes.** There must be a healthy balance. And so some lines must be drawn. If there is conviction in your spirit, you would do well to avoid it.

Anything that involves another person, having sex with an object, or hurting someone is inconsistent with God's idea for the husband and wife. Sadism is the practice that involves demeaning or hurting one's spouse for sexual pleasure. Masochism is the practice of receiving the humiliation or pain for sexual pleasure. These are clinical terms and indicate that there is a psychological condition that needs addressing. These acts usually involve whips and chains or other items. These acts and items **do not** glorify God. We absolutely should not bring this type of behavior into our bedrooms. A spouse who welcomes participation in such acts needs to seek deliverance. There is a spiritual problem present.

Having sex with objects or being sexually attracted to objects is unnatural. This is also a condition that needs to be addressed through deliverance. God intended female for male and male for female. This goes against His plan for intimacy between a man and his wife.

In today's society, we have gotten so perverse that there is no way that we could address every sexual ill. The best thing to do when in question about a particular sexual activity is to be led by prayer. Secondly, search the Bible to see if there is a scripture prohibiting this particular act. Finally, we've created a list to help you test a particular act to make a godly decision.

Here are Biblical tests and their corresponding scriptures to help you make a godly decision.

- ✓ Test 1: A sexual act should only occur between a man and his wife. *Matthew 19:4-5*
- ✓ Test 2: Neither spouse should lust after anyone else. *Matthew 5:28*
- ✓ Test 3: A sexual act should not cause you to coerce your spouse to do something that she or he believes is sinful or harmful. *Romans 14:1,14*
- ✓ Test 4: You should not be addicted to or controlled by anything other than the Holy Spirit. *1 Corinthians 10:12, 10:23*
- ✓ Test 5: The sexual act should honor God and your spouse and never bring humiliation or pain. *Ephesians 5:29*
- ✓ Test 6: You should never follow the patterns of secular society. *Romans 12:2*

CHAPTER EIGHT
IS THAT RIGHT? (FAQ's)

-EIGHT-
IS THAT RIGHT? (FAQ's)

Wisdom is the principal thing; therefore get wisdom: and with all your getting, get understanding. Proverbs 4:7

In this chapter, we seek to answer the most popular questions that Christians often have. After reading this book if we have not answered your questions, feel free to contact us. Our email address is listed at the end of the book in our contact page. We want to make sure your mind has been settled about what is Biblical and what is not.

Question: "How often should a married couple have sex?"

Answer: The scriptures do not give us a number on how often a married couple should have sex; it does tell us that a couple is to abstain from sex only when it is a mutual decision. I Corinthians 7:5 tells us, "Do not deprive each other except by mutual consent and for a time, so that you may devote yourselves to prayer. Then come together again so that Satan will not tempt you because of your lack of self-control." So, mutual consent is the "rule" for how often a married couple should have sex. The "rule" is that abstaining from sex must be agreed upon, and that even when abstaining is agreed upon, it should only be for a short time.

We encourage couples to have sex as much as possible. That is going to depend on the desire of both spouses. If one spouse desires sex every day, and the other spouse once a month or less, they will have to lovingly and sacrificially agree to a compromise, some sort of middle ground.

Question: Is it acceptable to God for a husband and wife to have sex while the wife is menstruating ?

Answer: There are several Old Testament scriptures that forbid a man having sex with his wife during her monthly cycle (Leviticus 15:19, Leviticus 15:24 and Leviticus 20:18). If we follow the train of thought that married persons are unclean if they engage in sexual activity, then we would have to say that it is wrong to even touch a woman during her cycle. The Old Testament scriptures forbade man to even touch his wife or to touch something that a menstruating woman had touched. These laws do not apply to us today. We are no longer under the Old Testament ceremonial law (Romans 10:4; Galatians 3:24-26; Ephesians 2:15).

There is no longer a sacrificial system. Jesus' was the ultimate blood sacrifice. He paid the penalty for sins once and for all. So there is no biblical reason why a married couple cannot have sex during the wife's period. This would be subject to a couple's personal choice.

Question: Is oral sex permissible?

Answer: The Bible does NOT forbid oral sex between a husband and wife. In fact, Song of Solomon seems to encourage it. This act is also subject to a couple's preference. If one spouse wants oral sex and the other doesn't feel comfortable about it, then it should be off limits. Never ever seek your sexual pleasure at your mate's expense. Love is not selfish. Sometimes a spouse who was opposed to it early in the marriage may be willing to try it later in another season of the marriage. However he/she should not be coerced into it or made to feel guilty.

Question: Is anal sex permissible?

Answer: The reference that the Bible makes to anal sex is sodomy and it is strictly forbidden. Anal sex is also very unhealthy and not recommended by health professionals. Anal sex does increase the possibility of spreading disease and increases the chances of infection. This is in addition to pain that a woman is likely to receive from anal sex. The vagina is lined with a membrane which is designed to sustain the friction of penile thrusting, the anus is not. In fact, some experts believe the AIDS virus was released into the human race through lesions worn in the anal wall while homosexual men were having anal intercourse.

Question: Are sexual toys permitted in the bedroom?

Answer: Some toys are permissible. Others are not. The scripture does not specifically address sexual toys. However, you have to be especially careful when bringing other items into the bedroom. Keep in mind sex was created to encourage intimacy between the man and his wife. If the toy will interfere with intimacy between the husband and wife, a couple would do well to avoid it. Items like vibrators, whips, chains, etc. do indeed interfere with a couple's connection and also devalue the experience. These types of toys should be avoided. However if a toy enhances intimacy between the two, it would be okay, again if both agree. Acceptable toys would be board games, card games, etc.

Question: Is it okay for a wife to masturbate if her husband has a problem with premature ejaculation?

Answer: Masturbation is the stimulation or manipulation of one's own genitals especially to reach a climax. God said it was not good for man to be alone. So he created the woman for the man. Part of that reason was for sexual fulfillment. God thought of everything. If couples experience a problem in their bedroom, the husband can stimulate his wife and the wife can stimulate her husband. But it is not a good idea for a spouse to engage in stimulating himself/herself. A spouse could easily enjoy his/her own stimulation and see no need for the other spouse. Sex is for the two to become one, not to remain one alone.

Question: Are pornographic movies okay to watch if we both agree and watch it together?
Answer: Pornography is watching other people engage in sexual acts. God never intended that we would get enjoyment in this type of behavior. Our enjoyment should come from our own participation with our spouse; not watching someone else. It is sinful and engrafts images in our minds that are hard to erase. Sexual desire for a person who is not your spouse is lust. Pornography stirs up that spirit of lust (Romans 1:32).

Question: As a wife, I would love to experience an orgasm. Is there anything I can do?
Answer: First and foremost, we should pray about any problem in the relationship. God can change our situation. Ask your spouse to pray with you. Share with him, what some tips on what he can do to help. If there is no physical health condition present, Kegel exercises may be helpful for women who have persistent problems reaching orgasm. This basic exercise can be done anytime and anywhere. The muscles that stop the flow of urine are your pelvic muscles. Just squeeze your pelvic floor muscles as hard as you can, and hold them. Start by squeezing and holding for a count of 3-5 seconds, then release and relax for 5 seconds. Do this several times in a day. You should notice a change after a

few weeks. If not, you may need to explore other options.

Question: What birth control methods are scripturally acceptable?

    Answer: There are many birth control options for families today. When we look at what is and what is not acceptable, there are only a few that would not line up with scripture. The first one is the abortion pill, also called RU486. The sole purpose of this drug is to terminate an early pregnancy. Another method is The Morning After Pill which in some cases also terminates a pregnancy. Not only are using these methods in direct opposition to the command, "Thou shalt not kill" but they both have very dangerous side effects and could result in hospitalization and even death to the mother.

Question: We are an older couple and sometimes very dissatisfied with the sexual experience? What do you recommend?

    Answer: Keep asking questions. Keep exploring your options. Do not surrender your sex life. Talk to your doctor about your options. If wife's issue is vaginal dryness, purchase a lubricant. If husband is experiencing some erectile dysfunction, then make an appointment to visit your doctor. He can tell you what your options are. If there is vaginal pain, try other sexual positions. But do not give up. As you age, it may take more work to keep a healthy sex life, but it's certainly worth pursuing. Some things can be corrected with hormones or other medications.

Bio of Oscar & Crystal Jones

Oscar & Crystal Jones have been celebrating their covenant love affair for over 30 years. They have 7 children (which include 1 daughter- in-law and 1 son-in-law). They are the happy grandparents of 6.

Oscar & Crystal are both teachers by trade. They have both taught in the private and public sectors. Both have left the education system for full-time ministry.

Pastors Oscar & Crystal have a unique Aquila and Priscilla team ministry. They lavishly love the Lord and one another. God has coupled this into a special anointing and gifted them to be able to minister from the pulpit as one voice.

They are founders and overseers of **Marriage for a Lifetime Ministries** in Oakland, CA and Detroit, MI (since 1992); **Greater Works Family Ministries** in Detroit, MI (since 1998), and **Agape International Association of Churches and Para-churches** (since 2000).

The Joneses are trailblazers with a strong deliverance ministry. Through faith in Christ, they have seen many people healed, delivered, and set free through the power of Jesus Christ. They have also witnessed marriages restored and reconciled even after divorce.

These long-time honeymooners continue to

have a heart for families. The two are dedicated to repairing the
breaches in marriages and families. They have ministered at workshops, retreats, conferences and other special events all across the country, crossing denominational barriers. And most recently ministered to United States military couples in Rota, Spain.

The two have been featured guests on several radio and television broadcasts. They host a monthly teleconference where they discuss issues relevant to marriage and the family. They also host Couples Cafés at churches across the United States.

The couple has authored several books together and apart. *Extreme Money Makeover, No Longer A Dream: A Step by Step Guide to Writing Your First Book, Restore the Roar, The Newlywed Handbook, The S Word: What Submission Is Not, Ring Talks,* and *When the Vow Breaks.* They aspire to leave a legacy of hope and healing to marriages and families all over the world.

To book them for your marriage event, contact:

Marriage For A Lifetime Ministries
P.O. Box 24906
Oakland, CA 94623
Or
P.O. Box 19774
Detroit, MI 48219
website: www.marriage4alifetime.org
email: jones@marriage4alifetime.org
888.884.3556
Friend them on Facebook:
Marriage For A Lifetime Ministries
Follow them on Twitter: Marriage4ALife

Made in the USA
Columbia, SC
29 September 2023

23588548R00041